MEGA-COOL
MEGAFAUNA
Creatures of Ancient Skies
Anastasia Suen

Rourke
Educational Media

A Division of
Carson
Dellosa
Education

Bridges

BEFORE AND DURING READING ACTIVITIES

Before Reading: *Building Background Knowledge and Vocabulary*

Building background knowledge can help children process new information and build upon what they already know. Before reading a book, it is important to tap into what children already know about the topic. This will help them develop their vocabulary and increase their reading comprehension.

Questions and Activities to Build Background Knowledge:

1. Look at the front cover of the book and read the title. What do you think this book will be about?
2. What do you already know about this topic?
3. Take a book walk and skim the pages. Look at the table of contents, photographs, captions, and bold words. Did these text features give you any information or predictions about what you will read in this book?

Vocabulary: *Vocabulary Is Key to Reading Comprehension*

Use the following directions to prompt a conversation about each word.

- Read the vocabulary words.
- What comes to mind when you see each word?
- What do you think each word means?

Vocabulary Words:
- asymmetrical
- azhdarchids
- carnivores
- extinct
- fossil
- herbivores
- megafauna
- membranous
- omnivores
- pterosaurs

During Reading: *Reading for Meaning and Understanding*

To achieve deep comprehension of a book, children are encouraged to use close reading strategies. During reading, it is important to have children stop and make connections. These connections result in deeper analysis and understanding of a book.

 Close Reading a Text

During reading, have children stop and talk about the following:

- Any confusing parts
- Any unknown words
- Text to text, text to self, text to world connections
- The main idea in each chapter or heading

Encourage children to use context clues to determine the meaning of any unknown words. These strategies will help children learn to analyze the text more thoroughly as they read.

When you are finished reading this book, turn to the next-to-last page for Text-Dependent Questions and an Extension Activity.

Table of Contents

A life-size model of a Hatzegopteryx, a giant flying dinosaur, is displayed in front of the State Museum of Natural History in v, Germany.

Only three kinds of modern living things can fly on their own: insects, bats, and birds. In the ancient skies, however, there was another: **pterosaurs**! This word means "wing lizards." These giants took to the air long before humans were ever around. How do we know about ancient **megafauna**? It usually starts with people finding a **fossil**.

Romania

Dracula

In 2009, scientists discovered small pieces of preserved bones in Transylvania, Romania. The scientists determined that they belonged to a pterosaur with a wingspan of 39 feet (12 meters). They named it Hatzegopteryx, but they also nicknamed it "Dracula" after the famous Transylvanian vampire.

Ancient skies were once filled with animals much larger than the ones we see today.

In the ancient skies, creatures flew above land and sea. What did they see as they looked down long ago? Scientists say that 299 million to 273 million years ago, there was only one continent. They called it Pangaea. This continent was surrounded by an ocean they have named Panthalassa.

Over time, the land moved, and new continents formed. The oceans around these continents were given new names. Today, people recognize seven continents and five oceans.

Pangaea

North America

Europe

Asia

Africa

South America

Panthalassa

Antarctica

Australia

From One Ocean to Five
The Pacific Ocean, the Atlantic Ocean, the Arctic Ocean, and the Indian Ocean are the oldest named oceans. In 2000, the Southern Ocean (circling Antarctica) was named by the International Hydrographic Organization.

The World Today

Arctic Ocean

North America

Europe

Asia

Atlantic Ocean

Africa

South America

Pacific Ocean

Indian Ocean

Australia

Southern Ocean

Antarctica

How did creatures of the ancient skies grow into megafauna? Scientists say that ancient life didn't grow to a mega-size right away. Before the Mesozoic Era, most living things were small. Over time, however, more and better food became available. Creatures slowly grew larger and larger until some became mega-sized.

Ancient creatures ate different things. The ones that only ate plants were **herbivores**. The ones that ate other creatures were **carnivores**. Some ancient creatures ate everything. They were **omnivores**.

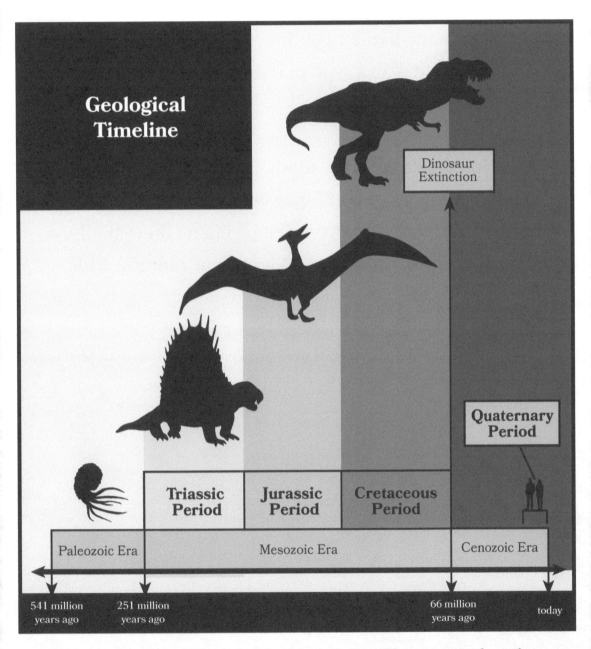

Geological Timeline

Dinosaur Extinction

Quaternary Period

| Triassic Period | Jurassic Period | Cretaceous Period |

| Paleozoic Era | Mesozoic Era | Cenozoic Era |

541 million years ago   251 million years ago   66 million years ago   today

You live in the Quaternary Period of the Cenozoic Era. The creatures from the ancient skies lived in the Mesozoic Era.

Herbivores of the Ancient Skies

In 2020, a paleontology student in England saw a fossil on her friend's kitchen table. It was a fossil of an animal's jawbone. The bone had lots of tiny holes in it. The student knew right away it was a type of flying animal called a tapejarid.

Tapejarids didn't have any teeth, and scientists think they ate fruit and nuts. They had fancy crests on their heads. Sometimes their crests were twice as big as their skulls. A tapejarid's wingspan could be 13 feet (four meters) wide.

Scientists think that tapejarids had very good vision, which helped them find food.

Found Around the World

The tapejarid fossil that the student found was originally discovered by a fossil hunter while he was walking his dog on the Isle of Wight. These fossils have also been found in Brazil, China, and Morocco.

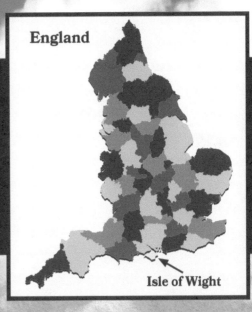

England

Isle of Wight

This tapejarid fossil has preserved foot pads, scales, and claws.

Carnivores of the Ancient Skies

Insects were the first animals to fly. The largest ancient flying insect was *Meganeura*, which means "large-nerved." Discovered in 1880, it was described and named by Charles Brongniart in 1885. This insect had a wingspan of 28 inches (71 centimeters). It ate other insects after catching them in the air like a hawk. *Meganeura* looked like a modern dragonfly, but it's much older.

Scientists say this **extinct** insect is a griffinfly. They lived between 317 and 247 million years ago.

Not all pterosaurs were the same size. Some were as small as sparrows. Others were the size of airplanes! Giant pterosaurs with long necks and bills like storks were called **azhdarchids**.

One of the largest azhdarchids, *Quetzalcoatlus*, was found in Texas in the 1970s. Its wingspan was 36 feet (11 meters). That's the same size as the wingspan of a Cessna 197 Skyhawk airplane, which can carry four people! *Quetzalcoatlus* was so big it could grab small dinosaurs to eat before returning to the sky.

Look Again!
In 2012, the History Museum of London solved a mystery. They looked again at a tiny piece of fossilized tooth that had been in the museum since 1884. They realized it was from Coloborhynchus capito, a rare pterosaur that had a wingspan of 23 feet (seven meters). Surprise!

Quetzalcoatlus, a pterosaur as big
as a plane, was named at the Aztec
feathered serpent god, Quetzalcoatl.

A second look at old bones led to the discovery of a new pterosaur in Alberta, Canada. For years, they thought this fossil was a *Quetzalcoatlus*. But when scientists looked more carefully, they could see it was a different creature. They named this giant pterosaur *Cryodrakon boreas*. It means "cold dragon of the north winds." This hunter with a long neck had a wingspan of 32 feet (10 meters). It ate small dinosaurs, lizards, and mammals.

Bigger than The King

Arambourgiania philadelphiae *had a neck that was 10 feet (three meters) long. That was almost double the length of other azhdarchids. Its wingspan was longer than a* Tyrannosaurus rex, *the famous "tyrant lizard king"!*

Some ancient life in the sky was similar to what you might see there today. When alive, *Anchiornis* had feathers, including fluffy feathers surrounding its body, earning it the name "near-bird." These creatures ate fish and lizards. They had a wingspan of 22 inches (55 centimeters), about the same size as a modern American Kestrel.

Unlike a bird, however, this dinosaur had four wings! At the end of each wing was a claw. This dinosaur did not fly because it did not flap its wings to lift off the ground. Instead, it glided. When *Anchiornis* spread out its wings, it could coast on the wind using its long tail to steer.

modern American Kestrel

No Longer the Missing Link

The most famous bird or bird relative is the Archaeopteryx. Discovered in 1861, it was once considered "the missing link" between dinosaurs and birds. As more fossils were found, scientists discovered more connections between dinosaurs and birds.

Two Names

At one time, Microraptor gui had two names. *It was also called Cryptovolans,* which means "hidden wing." *After finding hundreds of these fossils, scientists decided they were the same creature. Now it only has one name.*

Microraptor gui was another ancient flying animal with four wings. It ate mammals, fish, lizards, and birds. Some scientists consider it in the same group as modern birds.

The feathers on a *Microraptor gui* made it famous. It was the first dinosaur found with **asymmetrical** feathers on its back legs. Asymmetrical feathers help flying animals move through the air. This dinosaur used its wingspan of 3.3 feet (one meter) to glide. Birds also have asymmetrical feathers. This is one more example of how scientists are learning about the connections between modern birds and ancient animals.

The ancient bird *Argentavis* is the largest flying bird ever discovered. With a wingspan of 23 feet (seven meters), it was the size of a small airplane. Found in Argentina, it is a member of an extinct group of predatory birds called the teratorns, or "monster birds." Some scientists think this massive bird glided in the wind while it hunted armadillos and giant sloths. Others say it was like modern vultures and ate dead animals.

Argentavis might have swooped down from the sky to attack other megafauna.

1,000 Teeth

Some pterosaurs were toothless. Others had a few sharp teeth. Pterodaustro had 1,000 teeth in its bill! The lower teeth were extremely long and sharp like needles. The upper teeth were short and stubby.

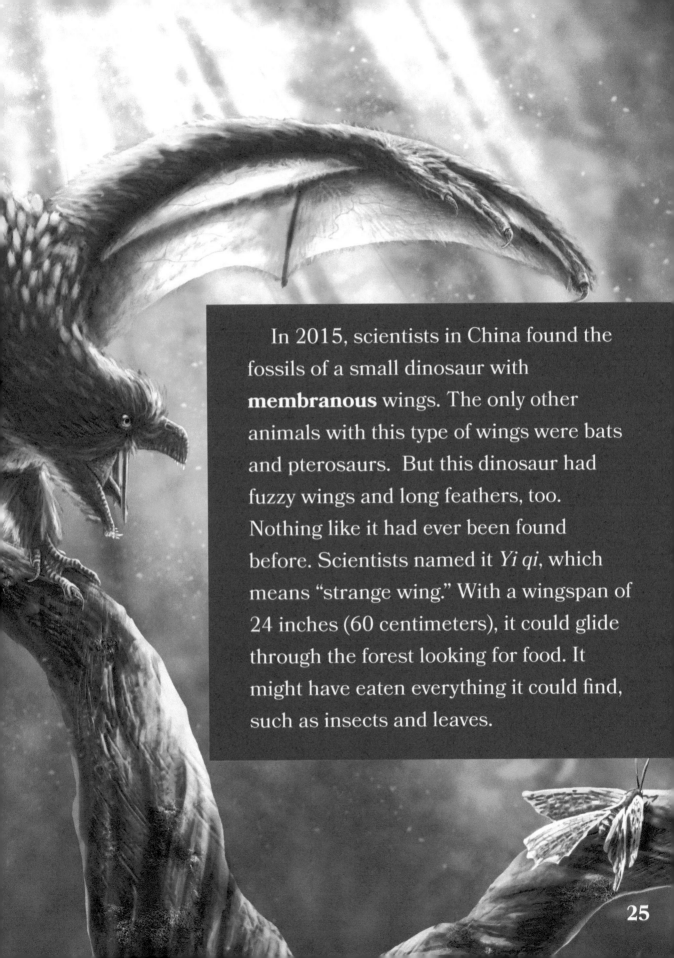

In 2015, scientists in China found the fossils of a small dinosaur with **membranous** wings. The only other animals with this type of wings were bats and pterosaurs. But this dinosaur had fuzzy wings and long feathers, too. Nothing like it had ever been found before. Scientists named it *Yi qi*, which means "strange wing." With a wingspan of 24 inches (60 centimeters), it could glide through the forest looking for food. It might have eaten everything it could find, such as insects and leaves.

Jeholornis was an ancient bird with two wings and two tails. Its smaller tail looks like the tail of a modern bird. The longer tail looks like the one on the four-winged dromaeosaur *Microraptor*. It also had the same wingspan (3.3 feet or one meter) as *Microraptor*. They both ate fish, but scientists also found seeds in the fossilized stomachs of the *Jeholornis*. This means that it was probably an omnivore.

From Big to Small

Scientists still don't know everything about ancient flying animals. New information and fossils are found all the time. Sometimes we learn more about fossils that have already been discovered. Old fossils might get new names or turn out to belong to a different animal. Who knows what scientists will find next? Maybe you will be the one who makes the next big discovery!

This fossil from the Shanghai Natural History Museum in China might still have more to teach us.

Today's largest ancient animal might not be tomorrow's. Scientists make their best guess about a creature's wingspan and other features based on the fossils they find. As more information is gathered, the names and numbers may change.

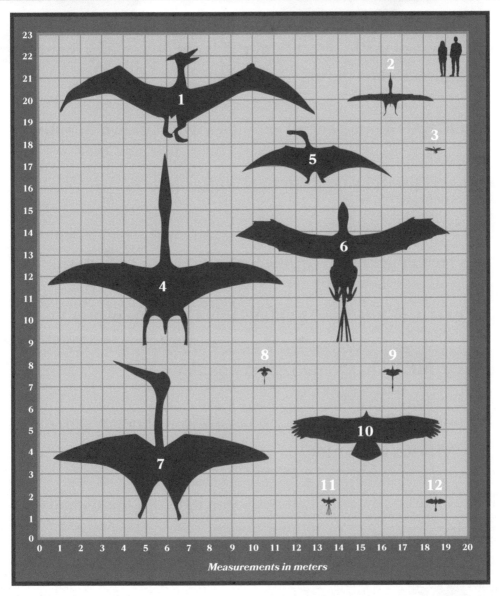

Measurements in meters

1. *Hatzegopteryx* 39 feet (12 meters)
2. tapejarid 13 feet (four meters)
3. *Meganeura* 28 inches (71 centimeter)
4. *Quetzalcoatlus* 36 feet (11 meters)
5. *Coloborhynchus capito* 23 feet (seven meters)
6. *Cryodrakon boreas* 32 feet (ten meters)
7. *Arambourgiania philadelphiae* 32 feet (ten meters)
8. *Anchiornis* 22 inches (55 centimeters)
9. *Microraptor gui* 3.3 feet (one meter)
10. *Argentavis* 23 feet (seven meters)
11. *Yi qi* 24 inches (60 centimeters)
12. *Jeholornis* 3.3 feet (one meter)

Glossary

asymmetrical (ay-suh-MET-rih-kuhl): having two sides or halves that are not the same

azhdarchids (as-DARK-idz): a family of large pterosaurs that lived in the late Cretaceous period

carnivores (KAHR-nuh-vawrz): animals that eat only other animals

extinct (ek-STINGKT): no longer existing

fossil (FOSS-uhl): the remains, impression, or trace of a living thing from a former geologic age, such as a skeleton or footprint

herbivores (HUR-buh-vawrz): animals that eat only plants

megafauna (MEG-uh-faw-nuh): giant animals

membranous (MEM-bruh-nuhs): having a thin sheet of skin or other tissue covering a body part

omnivores (OM-nuh-vawrz): animals that eat both plants and other animals

pterosaurs (TER-uh-sawrz): flying reptiles from the Jurassic and Cretaceous periods with membranous wings

Index

Text-Dependent Questions

1. What were the wings of flying megafauna covered with?

2. What do scientists think tapejarids ate?

3. What can happen when scientists take another look at fossils in their collections?

4. Why was the discovery of asymmetrical feathers on a fossil important?

5. Compare a creature of the ancient skies to one of today's flying creatures. How are they alike? How are they different?

Extension Activity

Humans studied flying creatures so they could build flying machines. Make a poster that compares a creature in the ancient sky to a glider, biplane, or airplane.

About the Author

Anastasia Suen is the author of more than 350 books for children, teens, and adults. She lives in the foothills of Northern California, where red-tailed hawks and great blue herons hunt for prey.

www.rourkeeducationalmedia.com

PHOTO CREDITS: cover: GettyImages / Warpaintcobra; page 3: Shutterstock; page 4: Uli Deck / dpa / picture-alliance / Newscom; page 5: GettyImages / dgero; page 6: GettyImages / ©CoreyFord; page 7: Shutterstock; page 8: GettyImages / Warpaintcobra; page 10: GettyImages / yanikap / DEA PICTURE LIBRARY Universal Images Group / Newscom; page 11: GettyImages / Wikipedia; page 12-13: MARK GARLICK / SCIENCE PHOTO LIBRARY / Science Photo Library / Newscom; page 14: Julian Stratenschulte / dpa / picture-alliance / Newscom; page 15: (inset) Shutterstock / Andrea Ferrari / NHPA /Photoshot / Newscom; page 17: Deviantart / Keenan Taylor; page 18: Matthew Studebaker / BIA / Minden Pictures / Newscom; page 19: Shutterstock / Dorling Kindersley Universal Images Group / Newscom; page 20-21: GettyImages / MR1805; page 22: Prehistoric Fauna; page 23: Shutterstock; page 24-25: Deviantart / © Rushelle Kucala; page 26-27: Deviantart / © Emily Willoughby; page 28: Shutterstock

Edited by: Tracie Santos
Cover and interior design by: Lynne Schwaner

Library of Congress PCN Data

Creatures of Ancient Skies / Anastasia Suen
(Mega-Cool Megafauna)
ISBN 978-1-73164-348-3 (hard cover)(alk. paper)
ISBN 978-1-73164-312-4 (soft cover)
ISBN 978-1-73164-380-3 (e-Book)
ISBN 978-1-73164-412-1 (ePub)
Library of Congress Control Number: 2020945086

Rourke Educational Media
Printed in the United States of America
02-0342313053